aries

march 21 • april 20

WHITE STAR PUBLISHERS

contents

Text by
Patrizia Troni

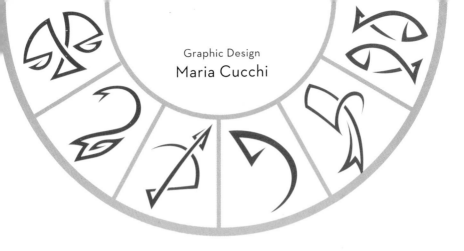

Graphic Design
Maria Cucchi

Character and Temperament

4 Aries

Aries have a spontaneous, impulsive nature that prefers immediate action to cold, rational reasoning. Their heart is pure and cannot contemplate any sort of deceit; they do not utilize subterfuge and double-dealing to further their ends. They like to excel, open new paths with rapid decision-making that grasps opportunities at once and immediately pursues the objective. Like Mars, the god of war symbolically associated with Aries, they are competitive, aggressive, with a magnetic fighting spirit, even bellicose, true warriors of light. While at times they are short-tempered and easily lose their self-control, ready to flare up, they are equally quick to defend, protect and help others, because although their behavior may be brusque and, at times, even harsh, their generous character leads them to do everything possible to aid those in need.

Their temperament is indomitable. They prefer to face people and situations openly and, if necessary, tackle them immediately, head-on.

Stubborn and obstinate, they have the spirit of the hero who always tries to move ahead, further on, and does not indulge in idleness and passiveness. Certainly, with all these qualities there also emerges the fault of a spirit that is sometimes too impulsive and that believes totally in a 'truth' it has found, without bothering to analyze it or view it with a critical eye. For that matter, Aries has no use for doubt and hesitation, preferring to make a mistake rather than fall into the quicksand of inertia.

They are exuberant, what stimulates them is passion, and if other people find it hard to share this great goal, they go ahead nonetheless, passing over all obstacles and barriers, breaking through walls, always moving forward.

They are vital, full of energy (what in the Far East they call yang). Tortuous, labyrinthine introspection is not for them. Their simple, direct nature avoids complicated tactics and strategy. They are filled with fire, determination and exceptional willpower that is expressed with un-yielding, steadfast perseverance. In certain moments, when the fire of passion is burning, they manifest unique audacity that, however, might also entail running risks. This uncompromising, impetuous stance could lead to a naïve lack of judgment, because they sometimes find it hard to understand what others, including those who oppose them, really feel and think and hence to deal with them.

Aries has a propensity for total independence, which sometimes isolates them from a social standpoint, and thus may result in others joining forces against them, or at least in their thinking that this is the case. But, they do not give in. They manage to do everything by themselves, they ask for no help from anybody, with the apparent self-assurance that aims at total self-sufficiency.

Together with their generosity and passionate heart, now and then they manifest signs of susceptibility, mistrust, and touchiness. They are self-centered. Basically, they believe only in themselves, which is a strong point in their favor, since they feed on this self-assurance.

They are also individualists – at times marvelously forceful and so energetic that they transmit their positive liveliness to the rest of the world, at other times a bit too arrogant and far too stubborn. But, when all is said and done, they are simple souls who wear their heart on their sleeves, so to speak. They are unable to pretend and their honest, natural spirit betrays frankness and sincerity that are yet other aspects of their fiery, passionate heart.

Aries is vibrant, impulsive, often brusque and rude, but their, often aggressive, nature must not obscure the essence of their nature, which is as clear and luminous as the sun in springtime.

Love and Passion

8 Aries

For Aries, love is fiery passion, a flash of lightning that suddenly sets everything on fire. Love is overwhelming and spontaneous; no reckoning, no cold reasoning, no subtle and prudent evaluation of possible consequences are involved here. Like life, love for Aries is a huge explosion that drags their soul, heart and flesh along with it. It is neither the head nor a purely sensual desire that govern their feelings; rather, it is the heart, which is ready here and now to give more than it receives.

Aries is male and active. And, in love, they act in an absolutely dynamic and extroverted manner. They do not play a waiting game, but move forward resolutely. When flirting, in the game of seduction, and in the dynamics of a couple in general, they are captivating. In a love relationship, they become a true driving force, an unstoppable motor with an exceptional spirit of initiative that overwhelms and stimulates their partner.

Although, in some cases, there is a desire for adventure, when they are in love, they see only the object of their love and nothing can distract them from this. Often when they fall in love, it is like a bomb exploding, suddenly triggered without any calculation or hesitation whatsoever. And, concerning seduction, they tend to be straightforward and

immediate. Once they begin they become overwhelming, tenacious, not at all affected by any initial resistance on the part of their beloved. They overcome all resistance; they conquer.

When love is born, it is a flame that immediately bursts and becomes uncontrollable. It burns and feeds on itself, but it does not always take in what lies in the shadows and hides in the uttermost depths of the other person's soul. A minor fault of Aries is that they sometimes do not pay enough attention to others' real needs. This denotes a basic ingenuousness that prevents them from discerning whether there is something unsaid or even devious in the other person.

This sudden explosion of passion may make it difficult to find the steady rhythm of a continuous relationship. The heartbeat of Aries has its highs and lows, momentary phases of tachycardia that blind them until the object of their love has been conquered. At times, love is something that comes and goes, that burns out and then blazes up again. This alternation means passing from moments of total generosity to others in which their strong ego is unreceptive to the subtle needs and desires of the other person. The concept of love as something rational, calculated and opportune is rather foreign to them. In its most rousing moments, this warm emotion becomes pure vitality, immense energy; it rises to incredible heights but may then slide into oscillating instability. For Aries, passion and love need strong emotions in order to blaze. Otherwise, they become a weak flame, embers smoldering in the ashes.

There is passion and enthusiasm in their heart, as well as a great deal of stubbornness and aggression. If the other person has an equally strong personality, a storm is brewing.

The strong ego in their nature may be wounded by disappointment. A broken heart transforms rejection or a crisis into excruciating pain that may trigger traces of sudden self-debasement stemming from the unconscious.

Their sexuality rejects cerebral complications, exhausting role-playing, delays, and suspended or long drawn-out situations. Once unleashed, their desire does not want to be stopped, and satisfaction is achieved through rapid and strong acceleration that goes right to the point, producing the sensation of absolute transport. While their imagination is by no means exceptional and their desire prefers not to beat about the bush, so to speak, they compensate for this with transport, strong and fiery eroticism that conquers their partner who will feel truly desired.

How to Hook an Aries and How to Let Them Go

If you want to conquer an Aries male then you must bear in mind that he is macho, a traditionalist and patriarchal. He is not the quarry, he is the hunter. For him women are to be desired, conquered and dominated. Therefore, it is best not to adopt a coy, mawkish approach or write love letters to him. Afterward, when the love story is well on its way, he will also know how to be romantic; but during the courtship he wants to be rapid, to 'pounce', kiss the woman suddenly and feel that she is totally his. The Aries male is a warrior, he likes to fight and struggle, so you should avoid both aggressive behavior and enervating shillyshallying. The key to winning him is to be sweet, attractive, reassuring, feminine, and wholly subject to his fascination. By caressing his head sensually, you will make him lose control more easily. Like her male counterpart, the Aries female does not like to be dominated. She wants to control the courtship, seduce and sweep the man off his feet at the first meeting. You should not expect timid glances and tender walks, hand-in-hand, from her. It is no use sitting on a bench with her like the lovers created by Raymond Peynet. Her motto is "Audacity's the thing." She does not wait for him to make the first move, but gets down to business right away, proposing, seducing and overwhelming the object of her desire, making him understand, point-blank, how strong her attraction is. There is no need for him to think about seducing her; it's enough to wait for her to do the seducing. Afterward, with a good dose of patience, she can be 'tamed' with kindness and sweetness.

You need only be clear, and to the point. Don't treat him or her like fragile porcelain. The Aries personality appreciates frankness; beating about the bush and emotional evasiveness are not for them. You need only speak openly, and say how you feel, bearing in mind that an Aries is stubborn. If necessary, you can explain your reasons then disappear as quickly as you can.

Compatibility with Other Signs

Theoretically, there are three Zodiac signs that are compatible Aries. There is an immediate correspondence with Leo and Sagittarius, fiery combinations that unleash instant desire, with rapid and total mutual understanding. When there is a common goal, the united forces of the Fire element explode and become irresistible. This is apparent in both work and romantic relationships. With Aries, splendid developments in the life of a couple are in store, although some contradictions may exist due to the mixture of such strong personalities. Other felicitous combinations are those with Gemini and Aquarius, which feed the Aries flame with their verve and their ability to communicate. Aquarius and Gemini help Aries to get about in the world; they restrain and guide their impetuous nature with subtle logic. Scorpio and Pisces are, perhaps, too sensitive and touchy to put up with those brusque and overbearing character traits that Aries sometimes cannot control, but they do appreciate their immensely generous and warm heart. Aries could have a long-lasting relationship with a Cancer partner, but only if intense emotions can prevail over their different ideas and sensitivities. The Earth signs Taurus, Virgo and Capricorn offer Aries the gifts of rationality and concreteness, which are useful in curbing certain ingenuous aspects of their nature. With the opposite sign, Libra, there are often fatal attractions as well as destabilizing misunderstandings. The energy of Aries allows a Libra to take courageous steps and eliminate the uncertainty that is always searching for the right choice, but in order to create a solid relationship the two must harmonize their rhythms and not become invasive and rash. Aries likes to makes a jumble of things, while Libra wants everything to be orderly. Therefore, Aries must come to an understanding in order to make the relationship develop.

Aries Profession and Career

For Aries, enthusiasm is also everything in their practical affairs and work. They must totally believe in what they do, because habitual, routine activities douse the sacred fire and reduce their interest to a dangerous level. They are like visionaries in their work; they set great goals for themselves, and are at their best when the effort becomes exciting and stirring.

Their powerful, overwhelming ego does not tolerate subordinate roles. They have the spirit of a leader, a general who inspires and leads his troops by setting an example in person. They possess a vitality that also becomes contagious in their professionwell. They impart a strength and a fighting spirit to all their collaborators and subordinates, and although at times they do not behave with the greatest delicacy and sensibility, they do manage to enthuse their colleagues, which ends up by tripling team strength and energy.

It is precisely their dynamic, vital nature that makes office work, and sedentary or repetitive work in general, unpleasant for them. They are pioneers, and in their profession, they like to open new paths, sometimes taking great risks, because they have conceived a vision or project that

must be pursued at all costs. At times, this pioneering spirit, the desire to make a foray into uncharted territory, which revels in sudden twists and turns, unexpectedly suffers from a loss of interest and a drop in constancy and regularity. In other words, for Aries, work often has ups and downs, phases of sudden great successes that alternate with others of decline or even stagnation. It must be said, however, that their character does not enjoy work experiences that are too peaceful and regular. A spirit like Aries cannot rest on its laurels, so to speak, waiting for a paycheck to arrive at the end of the month. No, Aries has to be carried away, to struggle, and, at times, even pursue impossible goals, because it is this context that stimulates their fighting nature to be at its best.

In general, Aries respects and has a high opinion of their immediate superior who must be deserving of that esteem. Even in the workplace, Aries is like a courageous young soldier who launches an audacious attack when spurred on and motivated by a fine commander. Likewise, they expect total obedience and commitment from those working under them; just as Aries is loyal, sincere and straightforward in saying what must be said, so they expect the same loyalty and sincerity from their colleagues and subordinates, without any beating about the bush and scheming. One aspect of their approach to work, that may sometimes turn into a defect, is their eagerness to achieve an immediate result. They don't like to waste time, nor do they like the exasperating sluggishness that takes days to deal with something that could be solved in a few hours. However, this rapid way of tackling problems may very well lead them to neglect certain details that, in the long run, prove to be important, or to make some unwise mistake. Too much self-confidence is a virtue, but can also be a fault.

While it is true that they are stubborn and sometimes break their necks over a difficult line of reasoning or a complicated question, at other times they decide to take the bull by the horns when dealing with something that really requires more patience.

Naturally, the professions compatible with Aries are military, especially positions of command. Aries make first-rate surgeons and entrepreneurs, particularly in firms with some connection to the world of sport. Other professions are those that deal in meat, hunting, fishing, and sports articles; they make good firefighters and, when there is some support from a favorable conjunction of their Earth planets, they also make excellent engineers.

How Aries Thinks and Reasons

They are also enthusiastic in their reasoning process. They are visionary, intuitive; they think that they have grasped the essence of a thing in a moment; they are convinced that no one could ever contradict them. Reflection, for Aries, is like a thunderbolt, a flash of lightning, a spark that, immediately, leads them to the heart of the truth. Were all this true, it would be undeniably formidable. But, in reality, their rapid, intuitive comprehension, which is always combined with passionate drive and impulse, is, subsequently, riven with doubt, or perhaps it is objective events that call their too deeply-rooted conclusions into question. It is then that they may suddenly knit their brows and pass through a phase of uncertainty and confusion in which everything that had been solved or achieved in an instant, as absolute truth, is now challenged and disputed. This gives rise to a process of analysis and reflection, carried out with highly rigorous and relentless logic, in which all the elements that must lead to that conclusion are tackled, individually, until the question has been solved definitively.

But, in general, for Aries, the process of understanding is not necessarily endless torture. Nuances, mysteries, and intricate dialectics do not interest them. Thought and reasoning must be the expression of a clear, simple truth, as clear and simple and distinct as the conclusions of the greatest rationalist in history, and the pillar of modern science, Descartes, who, by the way, was Aries.

With Aries, we are dealing with an intelligence that is capable of exceptional achievement and that can even open new paths and create new viewpoints, because their solitary, pioneering nature also works quite well in attaining intellectual results. They must not make the mistake of thinking that instinctive, passionate intelligence is less valid than cold, logical, rational intelligence. The problem is that they are sometimes too sure that what they have discerned, and the energy they invest in this process may turn out to be detrimental to the truth itself. Here we have an switch between the passionate, immediate pace of the visionary who is absolutely sure of what he has grasped, and the stubborn, suspicious and skeptical rationalist who, when all caught up in a certain type of reasoning in an absolute, intransigent way, ends up not admitting any discussion concerning what they consider to be indisputable.

Certain moments of 'empty logic' may become evident. Sudden obfuscation makes them wrinkle their brow, draw their glance toward the infinite and create a huge question mark in their mind. For that matter, this is the very essence of their nature: they get a running start and plunge headlong, only to find themselves, in the end, more often than not, alone and misunderstood. There are moments when they sense that they are not understood and are surrounded by those who have no intention of understanding them – a sensation so strong that it may create a clear-cut contrast. Thus, even as regards intelligence, ideas and reasoning, at times they find themselves alone against everyone else.

Another minor fault of their intelligence is that they see only themselves and their point of view, and have both a limited desire and a limited capacity to really listen to the deepest motivations behind others' thoughts. This results in conclusions that are, occasionally, too cold, stiff and abrupt, and which may give the mistaken impression of stubbornness rather than of a flexible mind. Fortunately, this is not exactly the case. Because, with time, they are able to lay aside the spontaneous simplicity of their heart and backtrack, thus triggering a process of self-analysis that is by no means superficial.

Sociability, Communication

and Friendship

It really is extraordinary to have a friend with the same Zodiac sign, because, while it is true that Aries is an individualist, somewhat solitary, and does not enjoy spending a lot of time chatting, it is equally true that they are capable of being affectionate with and dedicated to the people with whom they share their time and experiences. They make friends with that generous and spontaneous soul that is only too willing to be at their disposal if need be. Certainly, Aries - symbolically associated with the number 1, with the uniqueness of the individual, essentially independent, and, hence, individualist nature - prefer to solve things by themselves, to act and take the initiative personally without asking anything from others and, even more, without becoming involved in any enterprise in which teamwork is fundamental. The individualistic character of Aries has no intention whatsoever of being hemmed in by sociability that, for Aries, all too often becomes a means of concealing fear and weakness. Aries, who is audacious and courageous, does not want to have anything to do with the saying "in union there is strength." However, this does not mean that they are loners with whom a wonderful friendship is impossible. On the contrary, they give the best of themselves in friendship; when they are asked to lend a hand, they lend two.

At times, their obstinate behavior or certain brusque manners marked by curt, peremptory statements can create an obstacle to mutual understanding. Perhaps, in all human history, there has never been a diplomat born under Aries, because it must be said that the flexibility, adaptability and subtlety required by diplomacy are rather deficient in Aries. Again, sometimes their individualism makes their attempts at communicating seem too egocentric. Aries would not say "That person is nice", but might say "I like that person." The impetuous nature of Aries may lend a dizzying pace to certain moments of social life, but the first of the Fire signs is not particularly noted for its social curiosity. Their associations and acquaintances with people are incorporated into their individualism. On the other hand, one must not neglect a certain spirit of fellowship in their character that likes company and seeks the comradeship of other strong characters. Aries cannot bear weak people, moaners and whiners.

An accusation that is frequently leveled against them, from the standpoint of social relations in general and friendship in particular, is that they are not an example of great or absolute sensibility. While this is partly true, if we pay more attention to manners than to substance, we must not overlook the absolute simplicity of a good heart and the fact that their pugnacious and rather aggressive nature never bears a trace of malice, obscure viciousness or signs of betrayal. If, in some cases, they are insensitive, and, at times, somewhat pushy as well, there is no malice involved, and just as they are outspoken, others should be frank in return so that they will understand what must be understood. Should you have friends who are also Aries, then let them talk about themselves. The more scope you give to their intense, euphoric outbursts, the happier you will make them. But, don't expect them to return the favor and manifest the same patience; they are not world champion listeners.

When Aries Gets Angry

Bursts of anger from Aries are explosive; they burn everything around them like a volcanic eruption. But, just as quickly as they become angry, they calm down and the fire in them becomes embers ready to warm and reassure others. Often they are described as insensitive, but the truth is that they suffer if they see that their anger and fiery outbursts cause pain to others. Naturally, this does not prevent them from backsliding; indeed, they are quite ready and willing to go into a rage again despite their feeling so contrite about having done so just a short time ago. One thing that makes them angry is having to wait, which they detest, just as they loathe wasting time. They are the most active and immediate sign of the Zodiac, so that delaying, waiting and postponing are, for them, tantamount to passiveness, inertia, slowness and weakness. They fail to understand pusillanimous, uncertain, faint-hearted people. They are irritated by those who avoid situations. They have little sympathy for timidity, hesitation and intrigue. They demand frankness from others, not timid stammering and inexplicable hesitation.

Furthermore, people who oppose them head-on make them fly into a rage. They can be conquered by sweetness and gentleness. Those who have relations with Aries must explain the advantages and disadvantages of a situation calmly and clearly. They are noble-minded, generous, and ready to help those who ask for it courteously. But, if someone should shower them with peremptory orders – like a typical Aries! – they are ready for battle.

Symbolically, Aries is associated with military life. They have a high sense of honor and hierarchy and a respect for authority, which means that they don't bat an eyelid if what the other person says or does seems right. But, should they have any doubts, should they perceive a lack of loyalty and good faith in others, should they propose something that goes against their conscience and principles, not only will they get angry, they will break off all relations.

Aries Children

People born under the Aries sign are vivacious. And, when they are children, they are extremely lively. It is impossible to make them be still and quiet for more than ten minutes. They need to stand up, touch things, move around, and give free rein to their great energy that, like the magma of a volcano, is boiling inside. From they have an extremely exuberant character. Consequently, they find it easy to sleep when they are exhausted, but in their infancy during the Christmas period, they may have trouble falling asleep or may wake up in the middle of the night if there is no lovely, auspicious Moon in the birth chart. They are very sensitive (although they display this trait reluctantly), do not mind being cuddled and caressed and, in turn, are quite affectionate and tender with their parents. They love rough play and games in which they can show their mettle and distinguish themselves by excelling. They prefer to play outside but also enjoy themselves in the house if they can participate, do something or help out – in short, if they can apply themselves to some activity. What is important is that they are always able to move about. They tend to be obedient and they re-spect and follow their parents' suggestions; but they rebel against inexplicable impositions. They stoically accept punishment or limitations – after all, their character is fundamentally Spartan – but they will never accept anything they consider to be unfair. As far as their ed-ucation is concerned, it is best to give them 'guidelines' regarding their behavior, indicating a direction to be taken; but they should be free to act according to their own desires. Given their stubbornness, they understand something only after they have banged their heads

against a brick wall. However, their parents must see that these children do not waste their energy. With boys, parents should not worry about their being all neat and tidy, as impeccable as little lords. It is more than likely that their clothes will be dirty and their knees scraped. This is also true of girls, since they love to play the boys' games and even compete with them.

Music Associated

One of the greatest composers in the history of music, Johann Sebastian Bach, was born under Aries. The progression of his scales, which is overwhelming and marvelous, has a powerful, exhilarating, dizzying and electrifying pace that is analogous to the symbolism of Aries. If it is true that here we are in the most fiery and vehement part of the Zodiac, we are also in the area of absolutely captivating music, music that is by no means abstract or rarified. Three other very famous Aries are the great conductors Arturo Toscanini, Herbert Von Karajan and Mstislav Rostropovich. As you can see, their Fire sign really loves to conduct leading symphony orchestras. But this sign also boasts such rousing and enthralling composers as Béla Bartók and Franz Joseph Haydn. In the history of rock music, the Aries stars always communicate strength and vigor together with a warm spirit, features expressed wonderfully by such captivating singers as Aretha Franklin and Diana Ross. Because their music goes right to the heart

with Aries

of listeners and is anything but minimalist or metallic. Among the great interpreters of blues and rock are Amazon-like women of the utmost intensity, such as Celine Dion, Mariah Carey and above all Norah Jones. But, the splendid voice of the female warrior also includes the provocative, transgressive variations of Lady Gaga, who was also born under Aries.

However, all this does not mean that when they put on their headphones, in the splendid solitude that no one must disturb, they cannot also listen to sweet, delicate and magical music, which in fact helps to placate their archetypal ardor.

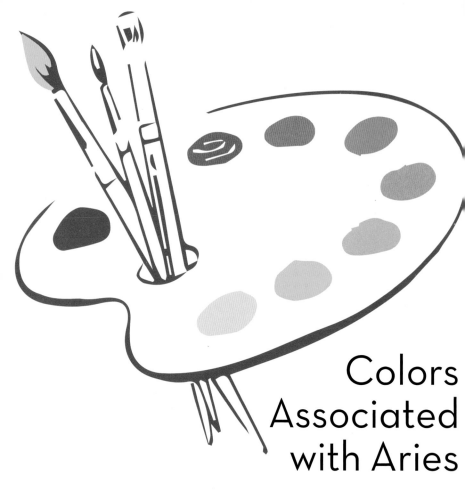

Colors
Associated
with Aries

Their color is red. This is a proud, conspicuous, ambitious color. A color that wants to be noticed, that wants to assert itself, to overshadow. A color that reminds one of fire and blood, war and ardor, love and hate, the flames of Hell and of purification, sin, and passion. Since ancient times it has been the most common, admired and sought-after color. It is a mark of distinction and power. Red clothes symbolize luck and honor, prestige, power and charisma. The army uniforms of the ancient Spartans were red, not to speak of the bricks of imperial Roman architecture and centurions' uniforms. Red was also the color of the god Mars' clothing. This is the red we find again in Aries, which best expresses in this color all its power, vigor, its pure and fiery spirit, its capacity to emerge and prevail.

Red, because every so often Aries "sees red" or "turns red with rage." Their explosive impulse is not always able to understand others' viewpoint, to accept compromise, to mediate. If they think that they are right then they become tough, unwavering, and monolithic. Yet behind their peremptory behavior is a heart ready to pardon and forget. They may explode easily but calm down just as quickly, and hardly ever bear a grudge.

Their aggressive and competitive nature is enhanced by the color scarlet. And, carmine is the shade of red suitable for seduction, as it makes them more audacious, sensual and irresistible. If they want to impose their ideas, the power of their personality, desires and viewpoint, then purple is the most appropriate color.

Coral is good for when they want to persuade, dissuade, melt or soothe someone, and burgundy to soften the mood, isolate or yield themselves in small doses. But, if they want to appear cold, solemn and detached, then they should choose Pompeian red. And, should they wish to restrain their aggression, be less stubborn and impulsive, or suppress their ego, then they should use rust red.

Flowers
and Plants
Associated
with Aries

The spring equinox marks the entrance of the Sun into the Aries constellation. Nature is reborn in all its luxuriance; the world becomes a blaze of colors; daisies, irises, tulips, jonquils, violets and forget-me-nots begin to bloom. Aries is fond of all spring flowers and certain Martian plants such as hawthorn (try to take a regenerating bath with a handful of hawthorn flowers in warm water) and hypericum (which is believed to induce prophetic dreams and ward off negative influences).

Every ten-day period benefits from a particular flower or plant.

First period (March 21-31): lavender. Its flowers are used not only to perfume drawers, chests and rooms, since lavender attenuates the aggressive nature of Aries and helps them to overcome anxieties, failures, contrasts and uncertainties without mortifying the typical Aries personality. If they undergo failure or humiliation, if something grieves them or triggers anxiety, then they should take a long bath, putting 11 drops of essential oil of lavender in the water, or steep lavender flowers in a sachet directly into the water. They will step out of the bathtub regenerated.

Second period (April 1-10): basil. This aromatic plant has an effect on one's emotions, helping to form clear thoughts and make important life decisions. Basil works a positive influence on, and attenuates touchy and distrustful personalities. It is advisable to rub basil leaves between one's fingers before a date or an important interview, because the essence absorbed by the skin imparts charisma, mystery and a magnetic fascination.

Third period (April 11-20): pepper. This spice strengthens character and triggers the right stimulus to achieve goals. In the past, people believed that carrying a sachet of basil kept them safe from intrigues, enemies and anything that created difficulty in life.

Animals Associated with Aries

Aries is usually associated with the ram, an animal that in many old cultures was the symbol of divinity. Amon-Ra had a ram's head, while Jupiter Ammon had its horns. In Vedic India, the ram is the mount of the god Agni, who, with his beneficent fire, gave heat and light to the cosmos. But, even more than the powerful ram, Aries is represented by animals that are symbols of battle, ferocity, bravery and war – first and foremost the wolf. Mars, the ruling Aries planet, was represented as a victorious warrior on a chariot drawn by two wolves. The wolf is synonymous with unbridled violence, savagery, and barely restrained power. But, this dark side also has its bright side: the wolf sees in the dark and hence drives away darkness, which makes this creature a symbol of the Sun and light in Nordic cultures. The wolf is also the symbol of fertility and protection. A she-wolf suckled the founders of Rome, Romulus and Remus. Genghis Khan and the Mongol dynasty descended from a blue wolf. Again, the wolf is the totem animal for Native Americans, their symbol of courage and a spirit of adaptation. One of their war songs goes as follows: "I am the solitary wolf, I wander about in different lands." Combative Aries, with a bold and loyal nature, is also represented by the horse, an archetypical animal that is deeply rooted in mankind's collective memory, connected to destructive, yet sustaining, fire and water. For psychoanalysts, this creature is one of the symbols of the subconscious mind.

Among birds, the woodpecker is the animal-symbol for Aries, as are such birds of prey as the eagle, the vulture, the sparrow hawk and the falcon. A woodpecker flew into Romulus and Remus' cave to feed them, which is the reason why this bird is sacred to Mars and is the emblem of protection and safety. And, for a tribe that lives in Malaysia, the Negrito Semang, the woodpecker is a sacred bird, a benefactor, in that it gave fire to mankind. Among fish associated with Aries are the pike and the barbel.

Gemstones Associated with Aries

Traditionally, the gems corresponding to Aries are red and the ruby, which is passionately red, is the stone that best matches the vital energy of Aries. Since ancient times, the ruby has been considered one of the most precious and perfect of stones; it is the bearer of vigor, perseverance, health and good luck, and is a great source of energy. In order to take advantage of this Aries should wear one near their heart or on their ring finger, glancing at it every so often. In ancient times, people believed that rubies lost their color when the wearer was in danger, and regained their original color when the danger had passed. On a psychological level, the ruby imparts security and confidence in one's capabilities, and also makes one more efficient and dynamic.

Red jasper works on the emotional nature of Aries and should be worn as a protection against becoming too involved in a situation or in dangerous or harmful relationships. Furthermore, it stabilizes impatience and instinctive strong reactions, reducing insecurity, fear, and feelings of guilt. Coral, whatever color it may be, also calms excitable Aries, relaxes their mind and, in general, increases the stability of their nature. In order to free the energy they have accumulated and to relax, it is best to wear coral like a necklace. Bloodstone is useful due to its blood-red color (the ancient Greeks thought it was solidified blood) and also because it has a high iron content, a typical Mars metal. It is an effective amulet against negative influences, strengthens perseverance and makes Aries more resolute and determined. It should be worn during work meetings and on all those occasions when an iron will is needed.

If they want to give themselves or another Aries a gem, then they should choose a very dark bloodstone, since it strengthens feelings and empathy. It is also perfect as a love token because it generates trust, attraction and empathy.

Best Food for Aries

Bear in mind that Aries is the hunters' sign. They may be diehard vegans or vegetarians, but them astrological DNA is decidedly carnivorous. The most satisfying food for them is game: partridge, rabbit, boar and pheasant. Barbecued meat is right for them, especially if eaten around an open fire with friends, as is everything piquant and that makes food savory, warms the heart and the senses: garlic, onion, shallot, leek, mustard, black pepper, hot pepper, and curry. When Aries cooks, they don't skimp on these ingredients, because not only do they make dishes tastier, but they are a fabulous mixture of therapeutic properties that are precious for health (we need only mention how garlic regulates blood pressure and lowers the cholesterol and triglyceride levels in the blood).

Nettle should also be a basic part of their diet. The plant that we tend to avoid as an irritating and stinging plant has anti-anemic and therapeutic properties for those who have iron and folic acid problems. It is rich in mineral salts and is an efficient detoxifying agent. Always gather it in meadows far from sources of pollution. Once it has been boiled, do not throw away the water because it can be used to massage the scalp as a natural remedy for dandruff and hair loss. Another suitable food for Aries is the fruit of the cornel tree, a plant rich in vitamin C, consecrated to Mars. The tree blooms from March to April and the fruit ripens from late August to late September. It can be eaten raw but is excellent when used to make jams, jellies or to flavor liqueurs.

Then there is the indispensable basil, which can be grown on a balcony, in the garden or bought at the local market. Its intense aroma is not only very agreeable, but, when added as an ingredient to dishes, provides Aries with energy, stabilizes their moods and imparts a pleasant sensation of omnipotence. Last of all, with lunch and dinner they should drink a robust red wine like garnet red Barolo.

Myths
Associated
with Aries

The red planet, Mars, rules Aries. For Aries, who is better qualified than Mars, the god of war, to symbolize and represent their courageous, dynamic, and impetuous spirit? Known as Nergal by the Sumerians, Ares by the Greeks, Tyr by the Germanic tribes and Mars by the Romans, he is the god of war, an intrepid god who dares and commands, who goes into battle and destroys, but who also knows how to protect and generate. In fact, Mars also represents the force of nature, fertility; he was invoked in spring during the ceremonies connected to the reawakening of nature.

Aries too, like the god, is ready to do battle if provoked, to tread the battlefield and rout the enemy. People born under Aries are passionate and impetuous when expressing their feelings, quick-tempered and touchy. Yet their violence is a healthy and vital drive that totally commits itself to achieving a goal. It is a vigorous energy that is willing to take responsibility for its actions, to expose itself, to lead, to fight and to protect those it loves. Mars symbolizes the authoritative, combative, overpowering part of the Aries personality.

Jason, the mythical hero who led the Argonauts on their quest for the Golden Fleece, represents the adventurous, penetrating, instinctive spirit of Aries, which needs strong emotions, and a goal to achieve. Like Jason, those born under Aries influence and persuade everyone with their enthusiasm; they are individualists but are also good at working with a team and at transmitting the spark of an idea to others.

They can also make the quest for the fleece of a magical Aries ram, and, whether it is a professional or sentimental objective they want to reach the result will always be the same. When tackling a goal, a problem or a challenge, they throw themselves completely, loyally and openly into the enterprise. In the Greek myth, Jason was aided by Medea. Family and friends are very important for Aries. Aries is independent, and solitude is no problem for them, but them inner flame needs to be nourished by others' flames.

Aries Fairy Tale

Aries is like Little Red Riding Hood, not only because red is a color that suits Aries to a T and is the color that best represents their personality, but also because she "was loved by everyone who looked at her," as the Grimm Brothers wrote. Similarly, it's easy for people to like Aries. It's easy to ask them to do a favor, entrust them with a task, because their generous heart will lead them to comply. And, they are easily noticed, because their dominating, irrepressible spirit leaves its mark wherever it goes. Like Little Red Riding Hood, they are courageous and impetuous. They are not afraid to walk through the forest and the wolf does not frighten them. They walk briskly, confidently and cheerfully along the paths of life. They illuminate the cold, treacherous and dark woods with their sunny, generous and dauntless spirit. Certainly, as this fairy tale teaches us, it is easy to dupe them and take advantage of their good nature, and this should be a warning to them not to expose themselves too much or bare their soul to others. In their work, family relationships and social relations, being an open book is not always advisable. But, just as Little Red Riding Hood and her grandmother emerged from the wolf's stomach unharmed, they will be able to get on their feet again, put things right, and deal successfully with every situation. However, unlike Little Red Riding Hood they don't need a lumberjack to help them. Seeing them ask for help or support is a rare event. They like to do things by themselves: they face life and its various situations alone and, if necessary, throw themselves headlong, flare up, and do battle. Like Little Red Riding Hood, they sometimes disobey and go their own way. They are self-reliant and love to do things by themselves; furthermore, they cannot tolerate impositions that limit their freedom of action. But, their disobedience is always within limits, because part of them is respectful of and is faithful to authority, which, therefore, makes them perfect for carrying out orders.

PATRIZIA TRONI, trained at the school of Marco Pesatori, writes the astrology columns for Italian magazines *Marie Claire* and *Telepiù*. She has worked in the most important astrology magazines (*Astra, Sirio, Astrella, Minima Astrologica*), she has edited and written the astrology supplement of *TV Sorrisi e Canzoni* and *Chi* for years, and she is an expert not only in contemporary astrology, but also in Arab and Renaissance astrology.

Photo Credits
Archivio White Star pages 28, 34, 38; artizarus/123RF page 20 center; Cihan Demirok/123RF pages 1, 2, 3, 4, 14, 30, 48; Yvette Fain/123RF page 46; file404/123RF page 16 bottom; Olexandr Kovernik/123RF page 42; Valerii Matviienko/123RF pages 8, 12; murphy81/Shutterstock page 44; Igor Nazarenko/123RF page 40; Michalis Panagiotidis/123RF pages 20, 21; tribalium123/123RF page 16; Maria Zaynullina/123RF page 36

WHITE STAR PUBLISHERS

WS White Star Publishers® is a registered trademark
property of De Agostini Libri S.p.A.

© 2015 De Agostini Libri S.p.A.
Via G. da Verrazano, 15 - 28100 Novara, Italy
www.whitestar.it - www.deagostini.it

Translation: Richard Pierce - Editing: Norman Gilligan

ISBN 978-88-544-0963-7
1 2 3 4 5 6   19 18 17 16 15

Printed in China